Cliché Your Way Through Life

Kids Edition

By:
Ciara Ward, LCSW, MSW, MCR, CAMS-II

Copyright © 2023 by Ciara Ward

All rights reserved. No part of this book may be reproduced, distributed, or transmitted in any form or by any means, including photocopying, recording, or other electronic or mechanical methods, without the prior written permission of the author, except in the case of brief quotations embodied in critical reviews and certain other noncommercial uses permitted by copyright law.

Illustrations: Leonardo A.I.

ISBN: 979-8-8689-5482-5
Imprint: Independently published

Acknowlegments

"To my children (Jeremy & Claire), your curiosity, imagination, and wisdom breathe life into these pages. Your ability to embrace life's truths has inspired me beyond words. Your laughter, questions, and enthusiasm remind me of everyday magic. You've taught me that clichés, when genuine, are powerful tools for growth and understanding. Your presence in my life is a reminder to embrace simplicity, practice empathy, and find joy in the journey.

You Can Catch More Flies with

"You can catch more flies with honey than vinegar" teaches you that being kind, understanding, and respectful often helps you get better results when interacting with other people. Just like how honey attracts flies, having a good attitude and being nice to people makes them more likely to want to help you or be your friend. So, if you're kind and friendly, most people will be more willing to listen and work with you. This makes your interactions easier and more fun.

Imagine you're at a playground and you want to make friends with the other kids. If you are kind and friendly, they will want to play with you and be your friend, just like if you gave them a sweet piece of honey. But being rude and saying rude things is like giving them sour vinegar. People don't like vinegar, so they might not want to be around you. Remember that being nice and treating others with kindness is like having a jar of honey that brings you friends and makes everyone happy to be around you.

Don't Cry Over Spilled Milk

Kids are often told "Don't cry over spilled milk" as a lesson in life. It means that you shouldn't get upset over small mistakes or accidents, like spilling milk, because everyone makes mistakes and has accidents. We are told not to worry about things you can't change, but to learn from your mistakes and keep a positive attitude. It's a reminder that it's better to focus on the present and find solutions than to get upset about small problems.

Imagine playing with your favorite toy and breaking a part of it by accident. You can feel a little sad because you loved that toy, but crying won't make it better. Instead, you should tell an adult what happened. They might be able to help you fix it or find a new toy to play with. The important thing is not to get too upset, because accidents happen, and there are ways to make things better.

When Life Gives you Lemons, Make Lemonade

When things don't go as planned, the saying "When life gives you lemons, make lemonade" can help you remember what to do. It's about turning lemons, which stand for problems or challenges, into something sweet and good, like lemonade. You don't have to be upset or give up when things are hard. Instead, you can use your creativity and determination to find solutions and make the best of bad situations. It's all about having a good attitude and turning bad times into something good.

Imagine you and your friends are playing outside on a sunny day and looking forward to a picnic. But then it starts to rain, ruining your plans for a picnic. That's kind of like when life gives you lemons: things come up that you didn't expect and might not make you happy. But guess what? You can turn things around, just like you can make lemonade from lemons. You and your friends could have a fun indoor picnic or play games together instead of being sad about the rain. Even when things don't go as planned, it's all about finding the good and making the best of any situation. That's like turning the lemons that life gives you into delicious lemonade.

Treat Others the Way You Want to be Treated

"Treat others the way you want to be treated" is like a golden rule for kids. It means that you should treat other people with kindness, respect, and care, just as you want them to treat you. Think about how happy you are when someone is nice to you. By being kind, you give that same feeling to other people. When you treat others the way you want to be treated, whether it's by sharing toys, listening when someone talks, or helping a friend, you make the world a better and friendlier place for everyone.

Imagine you and your friends are having a great time playing at the park. But then you hear two of your friends whispering and laughing, and you start to wonder if they're talking about you. How would you feel? Probably not very good. Now, think of a time when you felt left out or upset. You know how that feels, right? So, here's the thing: everyone wants to be treated nicely and included, just like you do. If you see someone feeling sad or left out, you can be a good friend by inviting them to play or just talking to them. Treat others with kindness, respect, and understanding because that's how you want to be treated. Everyone can have fun and feel good at the same time!

Think Outside the Box

"Thinking outside the box" is like a treasure hunt where kids use their imaginations to look beyond the obvious and find new possibilities. You don't have to do things the same way everyone else does. Instead, you can be creative and come up with new and interesting ways to do things that no one else has thought of. It's like turning a cardboard box into a spaceship or a castle. By thinking outside the box, you can bring out your creativity, find new ways to solve problems, and have a lot more fun as you learn and grow.

Picture yourself as an adventurer in a magical forest. Most people go in a certain direction, but you don't. You like to try out new paths and find things that are hidden. You don't stay in the same places. Instead, you look up in the trees and down on the ground. This is what it means to think outside the box. It's like being an adventurer in your own magical world and using your imagination to find exciting new things in unexpected places.

Birds of a Feather Flock Together

"Birds of a feather flock together" means that people usually hang out with people who are like them. It's like how birds of the same kind like to fly together because they have similar habits and interests. As you go through life, you might find that you often make friends with kids who like the same things as you or who like to do the same things. Just like with birds, it can be easy and fun to be with friends who are like you because you understand each other and have a lot in common.

Think about the group of friends you have at school. You and your friends are like a flock of friendly birds if you are always kind, respectful, and helpful to each other and to your teachers. You stay together because you make each other feel happy and safe. But if someone in your group is always making trouble or saying mean things, it's like having a bird in the flock that does not fly in the right direction. It could make your group look like they are causing trouble, and teachers could get the wrong idea. So, it's important to choose friends who are like friendly birds so you can all have a great time together and be known for being kind and respectful at school.

Don't Judge a Book by Its Cover

"Don't judge a book by its cover" is a good way to teach you to look deeper than what you see. People can have great stories and qualities that aren't obvious at first, just like a book's cover might not show what an exciting story is inside. By using this old saying, you can learn to see the good and unique things in everyone and to treat them with kindness and understanding instead of judging them based on how they look.

Imagine you meet a new friend at school who is wearing old clothes and has messy hair. At first glance, they might not look like the coolest person, but if you talk to them, you might find out that they're funny, kind, and do cool things in their spare time.

People can be surprising and wonderful if we give them a chance and get to know them better, just like a book with a plain cover might have the most exciting story inside. So, keep in mind that you shouldn't judge someone based on how they look. You might miss out on a great friendship adventure!

Knowledge is Power

"Knowledge is power" shows you that learning and understanding new things can give you more choices and abilities in life. Knowledge gives you the power to solve problems, make smart decisions, and explore the world around you with confidence, just like how superheroes gain new strengths and skills. It's like having a magic key that opens doors to exciting adventures and endless possibilities, helping you become strong, capable, and a confident person.

Picture yourself looking for treasure in a magical land. You need a special map to find the hidden treasure. This map is like knowledge because it shows you where to go and what to do. When you learn something new, it's like putting another piece on a map. The more pieces you have, the better you can explore the world and find amazing things. Just like having a complete map helps you find the treasure, knowing things helps you make good decisions, solve problems, and do amazing things. So, remember that you need knowledge to shine brightly and succeed in your adventures, just like a treasure hunter needs a map.

Laughter is the Best Medicine

"Laughter is the best medicine" means that you understand the power of joy and humor in every step of your journey. Just like medicine can make your body feel better, laughter can make you feel better in your heart and mind. It means finding joy in small things, laughing with friends, and looking for the good even when things are hard. So, remember laughter becomes a magical tool that helps you deal with problems, build strong relationships with others, and approach life with a positive and strong spirit.

Imagine that you're having a bad day at school, and nothing is going right for you. You feel a little down when you get home, but then your little brother starts telling jokes. You can't help but laugh out loud at how silly they are. Your bad mood starts to go away all of a sudden, and you start to feel much better. Laughter really does feel like a magic spell that turns frowns into smiles, just like a superhero's power can make things better. So, when you're feeling down, remember that a good laugh is like having your own superpower to make you feel better.

There's Light at the End of the Tunnel

The saying "There's light at the end of the tunnel" means to believe that things will get better after facing problems or going through hard times. It's a way of looking at life that reminds you that even when things seem hard, the future holds hope and good things. Just like you know that if you keep walking through a dark tunnel, you'll eventually see the light and things will get better. So, remember it's always a way to keep moving forward and stay hopeful, even if things are hard right now.

Life is a little bit like a roller coaster, where you might go through dark tunnels that make you feel a little scared. Things may seem hard or uncertain at times, like being in those tunnels. But guess what? At the end of the ride, there's always something bright and exciting. So, just keep going, and you'll find that there is a light at the end of the tunnel that will lead you to new adventures and fun surprises.

Be You

"Be you" is like putting on a unique outfit that no one else can wear. Just like your favorite clothes make you unique, so do your thoughts, feelings, and actions. When you embrace who you are, you are proud of your personality, skills, and feelings. Being you means fitting into the world in your own amazing way, just like a puzzle piece fits perfectly into its place. So, remember that being yourself is the coolest way to live, and it's a journey full of self-discovery, confidence, and lots of smiles!

Being you is like choosing your favorite color to paint with. Imagine a canvas waiting for your unique brushstrokes – whether you're a bold blue or a cheerful yellow, it's your choice. Just like that, being you means showing the world the colors of your personality and the light of your talents. When you embrace being you, you make the world a more vibrant place, spreading smiles and creativity wherever you go. So, just like your favorite color, let your true self shine through every day!

Milton Keynes UK
Ingram Content Group UK Ltd.
UKRC032045241123
433238UK00006B/80